CW00544623

NATIONAL EXPRESS:
THE JOURNEY OF
AN ICONIC BRAND

Peter Robinson

and

Harry Cameron

AMBERLEY

Acknowledgements

The authors would like to thank the following people for allowing us to use their images, record their stories and sharing their passion and enthusiasm.

National Express colleagues: Richard Ball, Simon Ingham, Blake Cotterill, Mike Lambden, Bryan Bannister, James Donnan, Paula Mitchell, Aman Garcha and Dave Wallington.

For use of their photos: Keith A. Jenkinson, Adrian Lees and Steve Butler (Secret Coach Park).

For sharing their stories and expertise: Adrian Lees, Richard Thomas and Simon Davies of Edwards Coaches; Caetano representatives Raquel Santos, Rui Rodrigues and Jorge Guedes; and Malcolm Keeley at Wythall Transport Museum.

First published 2022

Amberley Publishing
The Hill, Stroud
Gloucestershire, GL5 4EP

www.amberley-books.com

Copyright © Peter Robinson and Harry Cameron, 2022

The right of Peter Robinson and Harry Cameron to be identified as the Author of this work has been asserted in accordance with the Copyrights, Designs and Patents Act 1988.

ISBN 978 1 3981 1361 9 (print)
ISBN 978 1 3981 1362 6 (ebook)

All rights reserved. No part of this book may be reprinted or reproduced or utilised in any form or by any electronic, mechanical or other means, now known or hereafter invented, including photocopying and recording, or in any information storage or retrieval system, without the permission in writing from the Publishers.

British Library Cataloguing in Publication Data.
A catalogue record for this book is available from the British Library.

Origination by Amberley Publishing.
Printed in Great Britain.

Foreword

I'm immensely proud to be Managing Director of National Express as we celebrate fifty years behind the wheel.

We connect thousands of people every day. Whether it's to see friends and family, go on holiday, attend events or visit attractions; we've been helping make memories for half a decade.

There are very few brands that can boast such iconic status. The white coaches with our name emblazoned in red and blue are instantly recognisable and a familiar sight on roads the length and breadth of the UK.

Fifty years has seen a lot of change. Journeys are quicker and more reliable, our coaches are safer and more comfortable than ever, and we've continuously invested to ensure we have the greenest fleet on the road.

We will continue to improve what we do – from ways to buy a ticket to our on-board experience. But we'll never change our commitment to providing the best possible customer service when booking and travelling with National Express. I believe that's what makes us the nation's number one choice.

I'm excited to be part of National Express and what the future brings. I hope you enjoy reading about our journey so far.

Chris Hardy
Managing Director, National Express UK Coach

Contents

A Brief History of Bus and Coach Travel

The origins of the express coach routes that connect towns and cities across the UK can be traced back to the early stagecoach routes that began to operate in the early eighteenth century, with the first stagecoach company running a service between York and London in 1706. As the popularity of these services grew, coaching inns became early transport hubs, providing departure and arrival points and overnight stays for weary travellers. The development of specific routes also helped improve the postal service, which had begun in 1635, with mail coaches offering a more secure method of delivery than the mail riders who were slow and often attacked by highwaymen.

Between 1706 and 1830, forty-two coach routes had been established, linking most towns and major cities in the UK. New developments in coach design, improvements in road construction and the development of toll roads helped to reduce journey times on many routes. In 1750 it took two days to travel from Cambridge to London, but by 1820 the journey time had been cut to under 7 hours. Despite these improvements the mail and stagecoach services could not compete with the arrival of the railways, and from 1830 onwards intercity mail and coach services gradually went into decline, with most major services disappearing by the mid-nineteenth century.

London to Brighton Stagecoach, 1822.

However, as towns and cities began to grow with industrialisation, there was more demand for transport systems that could complement the railways for moving the growing population around. Most ordinary people without a horse or a carriage had to walk. George Shillibeer, a coachbuilder and stable keeper in London, had seen a type of horse-drawn carriage in Paris that he thought would suit a commuter route in London between Paddington and the Bank of England. Shillibeer's Omnibus service in 1829 was different from the old stagecoach services as it did not need to be booked in advance; it had a set timetable, a conductor who took fares and it could be stopped and boarded anywhere along the route.

The 'omnibus' idea – Latin, meaning 'all' – caught on and by 1832 there were 400 horse buses operating in London. This growth in the number of operators and bus routes led to significant developments in how buses operated; for example, the creation of different colour schemes for specific routes and agreements between operators on the number of buses operating on each route.

The development of the internal combustion engine soon meant that horse and motor buses were sharing space, and by 1904 services were being given numbers. Combined with horse trams and electric trams, cities were developing impressive public transport networks. Horse-drawn coaches and carriages (charabancs) also serviced the growing tourism demand the railways created in seaside resorts and rural picturesque towns, carrying passengers from the railway station to hotels and on sightseeing excursions.

There was an inevitability to the demise of horse-drawn services as motor vehicle construction and technology improved. The first motor bus to operate in London was in 1899. The early vehicles were not very reliable, but by 1904 practical and more sturdier buses began to operate, with the Milnes-Daimler and De Dion being the early manufacturers used by the London General Omnibus Company (LGOC) and Thomas Tilling. The London General Omnibus Company, a firm that dominated the London bus market, ended their last horse-drawn bus in 1911. Their competitor, Tilling's, ran the last horse-drawn bus in London in 1914.

107 LONDON. – Corner of Tottenham court Road. – LL.

Horse buses at work on the corner of Tottenham Court Road, London.

Charabanc operated by Epsom Coaches, a business that was to operate until 2017 and provided National Express services for a few years in late 2000s and early 2010s. (Steve Whiteway, Epsom Coaches Heritage)

As the larger bus operators began to use motorised buses, the operators of horse-drawn charabancs were also quick to adopt the new mechanised type of coaches. The basic chassis for these vehicles were supplied by famous names like Dennis, Leyland and Daimler, with the body built separately to meet requirements for adaptation for seasonal work. In winter the bodies could be converted for carrying freight. As technology improved the charabancs, which were often notoriously poorly constructed and not particularly safe, were gradually replaced with coaches that were designed for longer journeys – enclosed and fitted with higher quality seating and body work. In the interwar years the coach industry expanded rapidly, with many new entrants competing to run coach services between many towns and cities.

The 1930 Transport Act brought in a comprehensive new licensing system that decelerated this rapid expansion and limited competition. The legislation created an independent body of traffic commissioners who controlled vehicles, routes, drivers, fares and information on all services offered by all public service vehicles, and thus limited and controlled competition. This legislation, which remained in place for fifty years, is an important part of the National Express story.

To overcome the constraints of the 1930 Transport Act most operators had to reach agreements with competitors to share services and pool revenues. British Electric Traction (BET) and Tilling bought up many independent bus and coach operations. To further reduce unnecessary competition and maximise revenues some of the major companies formed an operators' association in 1934, Associated Motorways. Associated Motorways did not operate or own any coaches, but each member agreed their mileage of coach journeys and received an equal share in the profits. Founder members included Black & White Motorways, Red & White Services Ltd, Birmingham & Midland Motor Omnibus Co. Ltd, United Counties Omnibus Co. Ltd, Greyhound Motors Ltd and Elliot Brothers of Bournemouth Ltd. It is important to add that many of these companies were acquired in the 1930s by the larger bus companies, and became, in the main subsidiaries of BET, Red & White and Thomas Tilling Ltd. To facilitate longer-distance services operated by different firms, passengers needed somewhere to wait for coaches and to transfer between services. This led to the opening of the first coach stations – facilities that were to become an important part of the National Express story.

At the outbreak of war in 1939 coaches continued to operate and to provide a number of services, despite the inevitable risks and restrictions involved. By 1942, however, with the war deepening and no end in sight, and with fuel rationing in place, coach operators were forced to suspend their operations. The coach industry did not restart until 1946. It was mainly due to this hiatus in activity that there were so many post-war vehicles operating well into the 1960s.

Despite this, the years that followed the post-war austerity, the 1950s and 1960s, have often been described as the 'golden age' of coach and bus travel. During peak summer weekends Associated Motorways could have 800 coaches on the road, with many converging on Cheltenham where passengers changed to continue their journeys. While demand for leisure travel expanded, the Transport Act of 1947 has begun the process of nationalisation of the assets and operations of the major companies into what would become the National Bus Company.

From the 1950s the post-war period also saw the growth of international air travel and increased car ownership. Over the next twenty years coach operators continued to flourish, with many smaller firms being acquired by larger operators. Those involved in express travel started to look for new ways to retain and attract new customers. With the building of the motorways, express coach services would become faster and more frequent. In response, and keen to improve the passenger experience, Ribble's new Leyland Atlantean double-deck coach was designed with fifty reclining seats, an on-board toilet and an at-seat service, which soon became christened the 'Gay Hostess' service. These vehicles were easily recognisable in their cream and maroon livery.

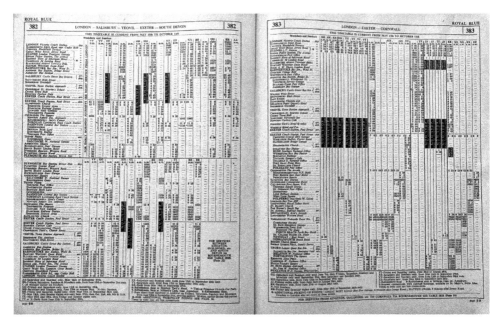

Express Coach timetables for services from Victoria, summer 1959. (National Express Archive)

The Gay Hostess service. (National
Express Archive)

1

The National Bus Company

The Transport Act of 1947 paved the way for the nationalisation of rail, bus and coach services. Under the 1945 Labour government's nationalisation programme the state began to acquire a large proportion of scheduled bus operators outside the major cities. Services such as those offered by Crosville from Birkenhead to Chester and Mid and North Wales were nationalised.

The Tilling Group of bus companies were nationalised in 1948 and placed under the control of the British Transport Commission (BTC), which was then succeeded in 1962 by the newly created, state-owned Transport Holding Company (THC). London Transport was also nationalised in 1948. Over the years that followed various private operators were acquired by THC.

However, it was a slow process of acquisitions, and it was not until 1967, when BET sold its twenty-five provincial bus companies and operations to the government, that most services had been nationalised. This final acquisition meant that 90 per cent of scheduled bus services in England and Wales were now under state control, with only a few smaller operators remaining. Yelloway was one such operator, though by 1976 they

The National Bus Company brochure. (National Express Archive)

had relinquished their express routes to London to the National Bus Company (NBC) in order to operate local Fylde coast routes.

This meant that famous firms such as Black & White Motorways, who were owned by BET, found themselves a part of the Labour government's plan for a national bus company. The government proposal had originally talked about creating regional transport authorities. The merger of THC and BET, however, offered a new opportunity, leading to a White Paper proposing the merger, bringing THC and BET undertakings into a single national bus company.

This White Paper formed the beginnings of the 1968 Transport Act, which created the National Bus Company. This new organisation was authorised to organise local bus services, working with the five regional Passenger Transport Executives (PTEs), which were under local authority control and the state-owned Scottish Bus Group.

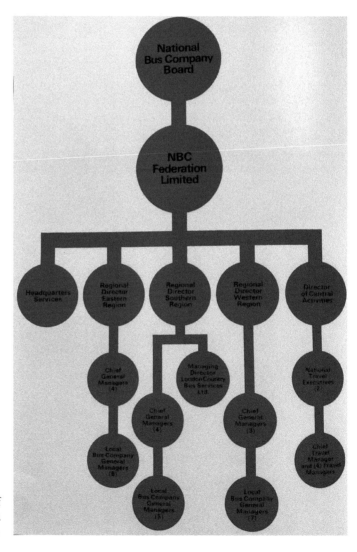

The original structure of the National Bus Company. (National Express Archive)

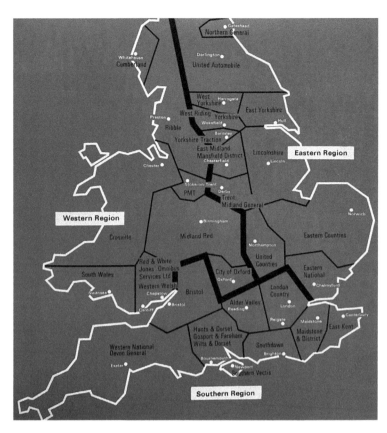

Left: Organisation of the National Bus Company. (National Express Archive)

Below: Preserved ECW-bodied Bristol RELH Series 2 – seen in early National Express livery and operated by Crosville.

By the end of the 1970s almost all of the company's original liveries had been changed to a simple corporate identity, with a NBC nationwide livery policy of Poppy Red or Leaf Green. Along with a corporate identity came the standardisation of vehicle types that were used.

In 1969 NBC had formed a joint venture with British Leyland Motor Corporation (the 25 per cent owner of Bristol and Eastern Coach Works, ECW), which in the process allowed British Leyland to become a 50 per cent owner of the NBC's manufacturing companies. The joint venture designed and built a new single-deck bus, the Leyland National, and a new double-deck bus, the Bristol VRT.

Leyland also produced an alternative double-deck in shape of the Leyland Atlantean, which was later superseded by the Leyland Olympian. For the coach fleet NBC were particularly interested in the Leyland Leopard chassis, and most vehicles in the fleet were based on these underpinnings by the mid-1970s.

Preserved London Country Leyland National in NBC livery.

Now in preservation, this Leyland National was converted for use as a mobile conference centre. (Keith A. Jenkinson)

Preserved 1982, this Leyland Atlantean is in Blackpool Transport livery. (National Express Archive)

This list provides an overview of the original bus operating subsidiaries of the National Bus Company in 1970, with subsidiaries shown below the holding company:

- Aldershot & District
- Black & White Luxury Coaches
- Bristol Omnibus
  - o Cheltenham District (1969)
  - o Bath Services (1969)
- Crosville
- Cumberland
- Devon General
  - o Grey Cars*
- East Kent
- East Midland
- Eastern National
- East Yorkshire

- Eastern Counties
- Exeter Corporation
  - o Devon General (1970)
- Greenslades Tours Limited (coaches only)
- Hants & Dorset
  - o Shamrock and Rambler*
- Hebble (coaches only)
- Jones
- Lincolnshire
- London County
  - o Green Line*
- London Country (formed in 1970 from the country area services of London Transport)
- Maidstone & District
- Mansfield District
- Mexborough & Swinton – *absorbed by Yorkshire Traction, 1969*
- Midland General
  - o Notts & Derby (1953)*
- Midland Red (Birmingham and Midland Motor Omnibus Company)
  - o Stratford Blue (already a subsidiary by 1969)
- Neath & Cardiff Luxury Coaches
- Northern General
  - o Gateshead & District (already a subsidiary in 1969)
  - o Tynemouth and District Transport (already a subsidiary in 1969)
  - o Tyneside Omnibus Company (already a subsidiary in 1969)
  - o District (already a subsidiary in 1969)
  - o Wakefield's (1969)
  - o Venture Transport (1970)
- North Western
- City of Oxford Motor Services
- Potteries Motor Traction
- Provincial (Gosport & Fareham Omnibus Company) – *acquired from the Swaine Group, 1 January 1970*
- Red & White Services
- Rhondda
- Ribble
  - o Standerwick (already a coach-operating subsidiary by 1969)
- Samuelson (coaches only)
- Sheffield United Tours
- South Midland (coaches only)
- South Wales

- Southdown
  - o Brighton, Hove & District (1969)
- Southern Vectis
  - o Crinage's*
  - o Fountain Coaches*
- Thames Valley Traction
- Thomas Bros
- Tilling's Transport (NBC) Limited (coaches only)
- Timpson (Coaches only)
- Trent Motor Traction
- United Automobile Services
- United Counties
  - o Luton Corporation buses (1970)
- United Welsh
- West Riding
- West Yorkshire
- Western National
  - o Royal Blue*
  - o Southern National (fully absorbed in 1969)
- Western Welsh
- Wilts & Dorset
- Yorkshire Traction
  - o County Motors
- Yorkshire Woollen

*Fleet names and liveries retained from earlier acquisitions

2

National Express is Born

A key role for the National Bus Company was to develop and improve national long-distance coach travel. This would be achieved by bringing together all the coach services operated by the NBC's bus operating companies under one brand. In 1972, NBC established the brand 'National Travel' to co-ordinate these long-distance express coach services, and National Express was born.

Coaching Activities

To co-ordinate and develop its coaching activities in general and in particular to take over control of its purely coach operating companies such as Black and White Motorways, Sheffield United Tours, Timpson's and others, NBC formed a Central Activities Group which in turn set up a new company in 1972 known as National Travel (NBC) Ltd. Besides responsibilities in connection with the operation and marketing of the 'National' express coach network, this company also provides the central direction for 'National' coach holidays and certain other commercial activities. It is also responsible for running Victoria Coach Station, the main London terminal.

To provide day-to-day management for its nation-wide operations, the country has been divided into five areas, each with an Area Manager supported by an Operations Manager to implement tactical plans, and sales and marketing officers.

Evidence of the vast scope of these coaching activities may be seen on our roads in the ever increasing numbers of coaches in distinctive white livery which carry a blue and red symbol and the boldly lettered name 'National'.

The comfortable seating of modern vehicles contributes much to the popularity of coach travel.

This sales office at Blackpool reflects the emphasis placed on maintaining the Group's corporate identity.

The original National Bus Company profile explains the vision for coaching activities. (National Express Archive)

As part of this consolidation a Central Activities Group was established in 1972 to promote leisure travel. The word 'Express' was added to the 'National' livery in 1974. In 1976, National Holidays was established to promote coach tours and in 1977 it became part of the National Travel Group, which would replace the earlier Central Activities Group.

Despite the improvements the motorways had brought to schedules, more competition from revived BR InterCity services, new faster trains like the Class 43 (the InterCity 125) and increased car ownership were contributing factors to the overall impression of inter-city coach travel as a downmarket and much less attractive travel option.

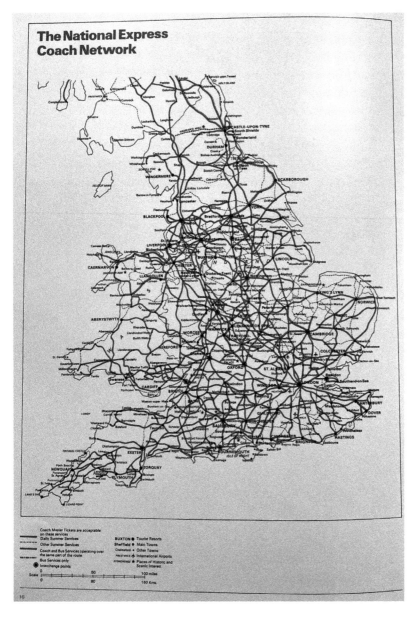

1972 saw the production of a national coach guide featuring all express coach routes across the UK. (National Express Archive)

The state-run National Bus Company was the biggest operator of express coach services, and a key role was to develop and improve national coach travel by combining the coach services operated by the NBC's bus operating companies under one brand. This process of unifying NBC's express services and shifting the image of the inter-city coach began with the appointment of Frederick Wood as chairman in 1971 (knighted in 1977). He had been appointed by the Conservative government of Edward Heath to make NBC a more 'commercial organisation'.

After the war, Wood worked in the United States until 1953, travelling on the extensive network of silver Greyhound coaches during his time there. What had impressed him was the reliability of services and the strong uniform branding that was used by Greyhound lines. So, with this challenge to improve the image of coach travel in the UK, Wood began to work out how to adopt the Greyhound approach in the UK, and he appointed leading graphic designer Norman Wilson to start developing an NBC corporate identity. Chapter 3 explores the National Express brand story.

National call centre, 1974. (National Express Archive)

All aboard! A National Express coach in 1975. (National Express Archive)

New style uniforms have been designed for National Bus Company's female counter staff as part of its corporate identity policy. Here we have Debbie Peacock (left) and Gloria Murray wearing two of the prototype uniforms which are currently undergoing wearer-trials in selected offices through the country. The ensemble, which was designed by the fashion students at Manchester Polytechnic as a project, consists of a coat, knee-length skirt, blouse and scarf. Colouring is predominantly red and white with a touch of blue.

New uniforms were introduced in 1975. (National Express Archive)

Although it was taking time to encourage people both inside and outside NBC to embrace the new branding, the new business was starting to attract interest from the press. In 1975 a story ran in the national press about a visit by that year's Miss World winner, Wilnelia Merced, to Cheltenham coach station. The police had been made aware of an alleged kidnap attempt and were among the crowd waiting for Miss World to arrive on-board a National Express service. The day was ultimately uneventful, with the paper reporting:

Miss World flagged out the 14:30 departures ... then climbed aboard the 'Miss World' National coach to try her hand at the wheel. With staff and pressmen furiously taking photographs Miss World drove around the station with all the aplomb of a 25-year medal holder. Afterwards the delighted dusky maid said 'I'm used to driving cars with automatic gearboxes. I thought I would never be able to drive a coach, but it made me feel very important'.

By 1978 the following bus-operating companies existed:

- Alder Valley – formed 1 January 1972 from Aldershot & District and Thames Valley
- Bristol – absorbed Cheltenham District Traction in 1975, separate 'Cheltenham' fleet name retained
- Crosville
- Cumberland
- Devon General – became subsidiary of Western National in 1971
- East Kent
- East Midland – absorbed Mansfield District in 1975, separate 'Mansfield' fleet name retained
- East Yorkshire
- Eastern Counties
- Eastern National
- Hants & Dorset – absorbed Wilts & Dorset in 1972
- Jones – finally absorbed by National Welsh in 1980
- Lincolnshire
- London Country
- Maidstone & District
- Midland Red (Birmingham & Midland Motor Omnibus Company) – absorbed Stratford Blue in 1971
- National Travel London – formed 1974 from Samuelson, Timpson's and Tillings (as National Travel South East), renamed 1978
- National Travel East - formed 1973 (as National Travel North East) from Hebble, Sheffield United Tours. Renamed 1977
- National Travel South West – formed 1973 from Black & White, Greenslades, Grey Cars
- National Travel West formed 1977 from National Travel North West (formed in 1974 from Standerwick) and National Travel Midlands (formed in 1973 from part of former South Midland)
- National Welsh – formed in 1978 from Western Welsh, which had absorbed Rhondda in 1971 and Red & White

- Northern General – absorbed Sunderland District, Tynemouth & District, Venture in 1975; absorbed Tyneside, Gateshead & District in 1976
- Oxford (City of Oxford Motor Services) – absorbed South Midland in January 1971
- Potteries Motor Traction
- Provincial (Gosport and Fareham Omnibus Company)
- Ribble
- South Wales – absorbed Neath & Cardiff, Thomas Bros, United Welsh in 1971
- Southdown – absorbed Brighton, Hove & District in March 1974
- Southern Vectis
- Trent Motor Traction, absorbed Midland General in 1971
- United Automobile Services
- United Counties
- West Riding
- West Yorkshire
- Western National
- Yorkshire Traction
- Yorkshire Woollen – under West Riding management

3

Branding and Design

Companies and service organisations have the same problem of identity as individual people. They act in a particular way, and their 'dress', i.e., public visual appearance, should amplify their character, or intended character. This 'dress' will of course only enhance the actual image which exists in the public mind due to the actions of that company.

The need, therefore, arises to establish what the identity is or should be, and to establish how to convey it in terms which adequately reflect it through all visual activities. A cumulative effect is produced which is inter-related and consciously organised.

Norman Wilson, 1973

The *Marketing Strategy Manual*.
(National Express Archive)

The creation of the National Bus Company was seen by many as a sad day, not because of the creation of the new nationalised operator, but because of the loss of so many of the well-recognised and colourful liveries of the time.

Of course, it was inevitable that this new operation needed to develop a clear brand identity. This was seen as so critical that the incoming NBC Chair, Freddie Wood, had already invited Norman Wilson (1931–91), the designer who reinvented the Croda International brand for Wood when he was CEO of that organisation, to develop some ideas. During the 1970s Wilson's reputation grew as Manchester's leading graphic designer.

Wood's preference was to create a simple, bold, and modern design using carefully chosen colours, fonts and images to assert NBC as a nationally recognised operator. He had originally planned to adopt the Greyhound approach of shiny bare metal but was persuaded that this approach was incompatible with British weather. As his design ideas evolved, NBC developed their *Corporate Identity Manual*, which showed how the new logo should be applied to each vehicle. There remained many in the industry, including some of the senior NBC team who were still reluctant to adopt a centralised approach to branding. Outside the organisation, there was a great deal of anger and scepticism around the use of the corporate all-white livery by the subsidiary coach companies, as it brought to an end the use of the popular local liveries that had been created in the early days of coach travel.

Many directors sought to delay the implementation of the new design standards as a low-key protest to be allowed more autonomy. Operators also objected to all-over white on the grounds that they would show dirt. Wilson retorted, in a characteristically blunt fashion, that 'they'll just have to wash them more often then, won't they?'.

The adoption of the NBC brand 'National' on all coaches was also not without controversy and compromises were made to allow subsidiaries to have local company fleet names applied on National coaches above the front wheel arch.

The National Express branding guidelines. (National Express Archive)

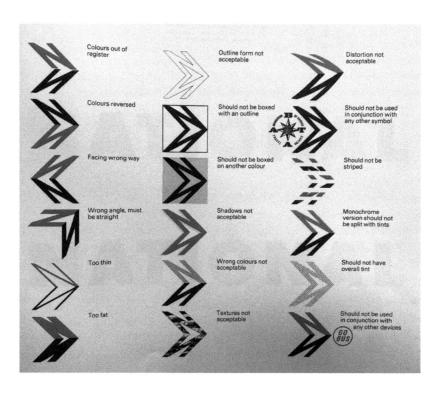

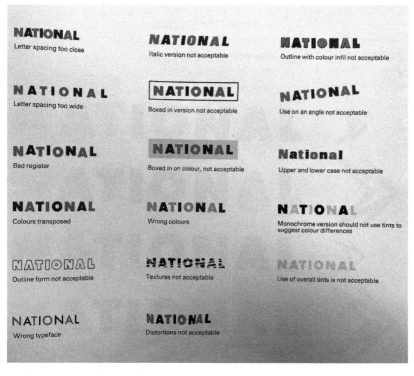

The National Express branding guidelines. (National Express Archive)

By 1973 Wood and Wilson had won the debate, and NBC design standards were applied across the business. This was not, of course, the end of the branding story. This was critical to the firm's success, because NBC was essentially a branding and management activity coordinating the activities of a number of major operators.

In 1974, to differentiate the express coach services, the word 'Express' was added after the National logo. Individual subsidiaries' names were dropped from the liveries in 1976 and the white and blue stripes were added in 1978. At the same time the National Express brand was applied to the entire NBC fleet. 1978 also saw the creation of branded booking offices at major travel hubs. At this time adverts were occasionally added to the rear of vehicles promoting particular route fares and the Flightlink and Jetlink brands were created for routes to Heathrow, Gatwick and Luton airports.

The next major change to branding came in 1981. The Rapide brand represented a new standard in coach travel with fewer seats, more legroom, on-board toilet and galley and a hostess service. Most services terminated in London, although there were a number of cross-country routes.

These new services were accompanied with some further design changes. 1983 saw the further refinement of the blue and red stripes used on vehicles, with a diagonal set of lines behind the front wheel in alternative colours. These were referred to as 'speed stripes' or 'the venetian blinds' and were also reflected in the Rapide logo.

Although not discussed in detail in this book, local National Express services (buses rather than coaches) were also allowed to move away from the Poppy Red and Leaf Green and white colours that had been used since the early 1970s.

The National Express branding guidelines. (National Express Archive)

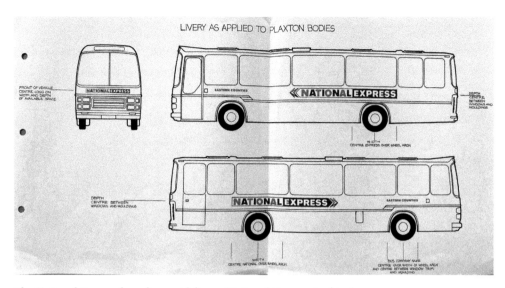

The National Express branding guidelines. (National Express Archive)

The National
Express
branding
guidelines.
(National
Express Archive)

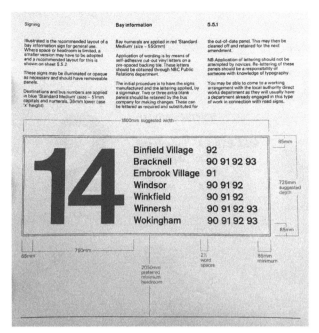

The National Express branding guidelines. (National Express Archive)

National Express branding in practice. (National Express Archive)

National Express Travel Office – showing branding and promotional materials.

National Express liveries in the 1980s. (National Express Archive)

Poppy Red NBC liveries. (National Express Archive)

Early 1980s marketing materials used in promotion of National Express services.

Towards the end of the 1990s the business began to focus on the opportunities presented by the internet to drive business and attract new markets. In 2000 Rapide disappeared, to be replaced by the new GoByCoach.com branding and, in 2003, the company name was rewritten in lower case letter, retaining a capital N and E and supported with a new circle design and white arrow.

This bold new design was part of a major brand overhaul led by CEO Dennis Wormwell: 'The logo, which represents connections between people and places, and incorporates the hint of a smile, is designed to rejuvenate the brand.'

In the 1990s, with the acquisition of companies including Eurolines (1993), East Midlands Airport (1993) and West Midlands Travel 1995), and two successful rail franchise bids (Midland Mainline and Gatwick Express), the business was managing multiple brands. Rebranding West Midlands Travel as Travel West Midlands, and creating Travel Coventry as a spin out, created further brand complexity. The Travel... brand was developed further with the creation of Travel Dundee and the acquisition of Tellings Golden Miller, which was then branded Travel London.

In 2007, with further rail franchise operations joining the fold, the business announced plans to rebrand all these constituent companies under a new unified National Express identity, led by the iconic Wilson evolved National Express design that had, until this date, only been used on the coach division. That this was the choice for the overarching brand says much about the success and longevity of Wilson's work and the public recognition and value associated with the brand. This is, of course, a direct consequence of the firm's presence across the UK through its express coach services.

Plaxton Paragon with 'Go By Coach' branding. (National Express)

Caetano Levante with the Dennis Wormwell-era branding. (National Express)

Plaxton Premier in Eurolines livery. (National Express)

More than just a branding exercise, the rebrand coincided with the appointment of a group director for all UK operations, bringing operational and strategic activities together.

This new design, which retained Wilson's original colour pallet, saw the introduction of a new rounded typeface and the inclusion of the grey diagonal parallel lines with round ends, which symbolise connections and punctuality. Sub-brands, such as the East Anglia rail franchise, are identified with sub-headings, though this was not applied in every instance. It also saw the introduction of a new, brighter white, replacing the slightly creamy white used for many years.

Since 2015 the grey lines, which were also related to the rail business, have been removed from the vehicle livery, leaving clean, lower-case blue and red National Express font.

Interestingly, this policy was not applied to the December 2007 purchase of the Kent-based Kings Ferry Travel Group, which continues to operate coach hire activities in original livery. This was also the year that National Express became Wembley Stadium's official travel partner and a Wembley logo was added to all the vehicles in the fleet.

National Express livery applied to rail rolling stock. (Simon Ingham)

Left: In 2007, National Express became Wembley Stadium's official travel partner.

Below: The Kings Ferry marked the Queen's birthday by temporarily changing the branding on some vehicles to 'Queens Ferry'. (Simon Ingham)

4

The 1980s: Privatisation and Management Buyouts

On 6 October 1980, Britain's coach services were deregulated. The Transport Act of 1980 dismantled most of the regulations that applied to express coach, excursion and tour operations in the UK that had been in existence since the 1930s.

The Road Traffic Act of 1930 had imposed the need for licences to operate coach services and introduced regulations on fares that were controlled by traffic commissioners, who also had the power to grant or block the road service licence that was required to operate a service. Any operator who wanted to operate a new service, run an excursion or a tour also had to justify the need for that service. Furthermore, anyone objecting to the new service could block the proposal and appeal to the traffic commissioners to stop the service running. These regulations had applied not only to scheduled services, which were controlled by mainly state-owned firms, but also to excursions and tours.

The ideology of the newly elected Conservative government in 1979 was to introduce free market principles, deregulation and privatisation of many nationalised industries. The 1980 Act allowed new entrants to the market (initially limited to offering a minimum shortest journey of 30 miles, but this was soon reduced to 15 and then removed altogether) and allowed those operators to run express services without needing to apply for a licence, without oversight from traffic commissioners and without giving existing operators the right to appeal against competition.

National Express provided the transport for the West Indies cricket team tour in 1980. (National Express Archive)

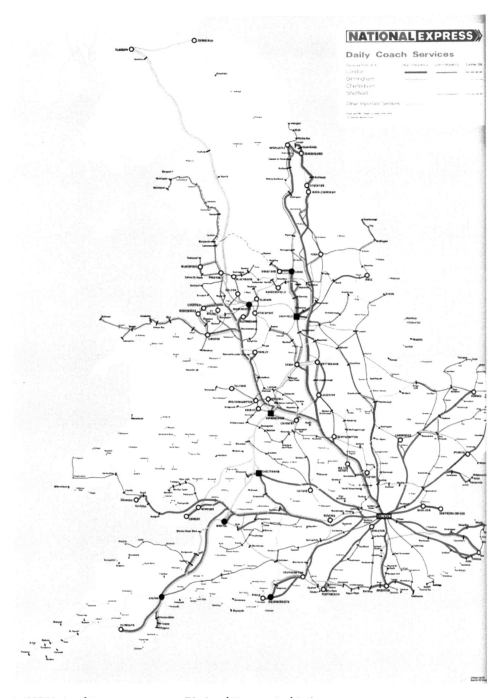

A 1982 National Express route map. (National Express Archive)

In a bid to win market share by competing on price, the British Coachways consortium was created, and comprised of a number of well-known operators including Wallace Arnold, Ellerman Beeline, Parks of Hamilton, Shearings-Ribberdale, Grey Green and Morris Bros of Swansea. As this partnership gained traction, other operators joined including Barton, Yorks Travel, Warner Fairfax and Excelsior of Bournemouth. An aggressive price war ensued, but the newly formed group struggled to gain ground against National Express.

It didn't help that while National Express enjoyed the facilities offered at Victoria coach station, British Coachways were providing a London terminus on vacant land behind St Pancras station. In the 1980s this was an area of the city in terminal post-industrial decline, an issue that wasn't addressed until the early 2000s with the development of High Speed 1.

By 1982, with operators pulling out of the partnership, British Coachways floundered and sank. The operators were simply unable to compete with the two state-owned operators (the National Bus Company, NBC, and the Scottish Bus Group, SBG), both of which had access to large fleets of vehicles and also owned the majority of the major coach and bus stations. Interestingly, the Excelsior operated route between London and Poole was the sole survivor and continued until 1998 when it was acquired by National Express.

This Volvo B58 coach with Plaxton bodywork was new to Morris Bros of Swansea in June 1981. It is now preserved in British Coachways livery. (Keith A. Jenkinson)

Some other independents did operate successful long-distance routes. Stagecoach, for example, entered the market in 1980, operating a service between Dundee and London, and, importantly for the National Express story, Trathens began operating a London to Plymouth route with a newly acquired Neoplan Skyliner. This was at a time when most UK operators were still relying on Plaxton Supreme and Duple Dominant fleets – both similar coaches that lacked many on-board facilities. Trathens also acquired Glennline and continued to operate their London to Exeter route. In 1981 they began working with National Express to offer the 'Rapide Shuttle' service with an on-board hostess serving food and drink.

Trathen's Rapide service, operated with a Neoplan Skyliner STT, leaving Victoria coach station with a National Express sign in the window. (Keith A. Jenkinson)

National Express owned and operated Neoplan on the M6. (National Express Archive)

This was only possible in part due to the design and specification of the Neoplan, a rare sight on British roads in 1980. The specification of many of the heavyweight European products from Bova, VanHool, Neoplan and Jonckeheere with their raised seating positions and on-board facilities made them attractive to UK operators seeking differentiation and improved passenger comfort. With passengers seated further away from any engine

Transport

Press Notice No: 387   **Date:** 10 November 1982

· 2 NOV 1982

CHALLENGE OF THE LUXURY COACH - DAVID HOWELL

"Transport operators must look to their laurels in order to meet the challenge of the luxury coach", David Howell, Secretary of State for Transport, said today.

Handing over the first British Leyland integral coach - known as the Royal Tiger Doyen - to National Express at Victoria Coach Station, London, Mr Howell said:

"This Government has done more than any other Government for a very long time to help the British coach industry.

"The success of the Transport Act 1980 is undeniable. It brought about an unparalled expansion of the market for inter-city coach travel; and by removing unnecessary bureaucratic restrictions it created the conditions in which enterprise could flourish.

"The real success of the 1980 Act, however, belongs not to the Government, but to the industry. It is the coach operator who has seized the new business opportunities, and given the public what they want. A whole new market for luxury coach travel has emerged. The bus itself is shaking off the 'bus image'. Coaches nowadays - and the Royal Tiger is a prime example - can offer all the luxuries we associate with air and first class rail travel. Expecially on motorway routes, they can offer speed and frequency.

"It is crystal clear to me that other operators are going to have to look to their laurels in order to meet the challenge of the luxury coach. No one is guaranteed a market share for all time - certainly not by me."

This press release from Mr David Howells, MP and Secretary of State for Transport 1981–83, illustrates the Conservative government's view that deregulation had been successful, but went on to highlight the importance of operators purchasing British-built coaches. (National Express Archive)

A 1986 Leyland Royal Tiger Doyen Rapide outside Midland House. (National Express Archive)

noise, they enjoyed a quieter and smoother ride. An inevitable consequence was the move away from older vehicles as operators sought to update their fleets. Plaxton responded with the Paramount, while Duple developed the Laser and the Caribbean, and Leyland launched the Royal Tiger Doyen.

> Classic elegance from Leyland. At last the coach everyone's been waiting for, a high floor, luxurious, powerful, rear engined integral coach with all the flair and style previously only seen in Europe - designed and built in Britain – by Leyland of course.
> Sales brochure, 1982

National Express could not deliver its full timetable with its own fleet of vehicles, so needed to work with NBC subsidiaries, who were paid 1p per seat per mile to deliver National Express routes. Keen to set standards, National Express reserved the right to inspect operators' vehicles to ensure they were suitable and delivered appropriate levels of passenger comfort. As independent operators increasingly invested in European vehicles and luxuriously appointed double-deckers, National Express commissioned Eastern Coach Works (ECW) to design a prototype double-decker on a Leyland Olympian chassis. Passenger feedback on the Bristol to London service where it operated was very positive and helped set the direction for future fleet investments.

The 1984 government White Paper summed up the new thinking on services and ownership. It stated, 'there is no good reason why local bus services should be provided by

A Salvador Caetano coach on a Leyland chassis, 1986. (National Express Archive)

a national corporation' and recommended that the National Bus Company be reorganised into smaller independent units, to be sold off as private companies.

With the Transport Act of 1985 the Conservative government could now achieve the end game for privatisation, by breaking up the National Bus Company and selling its seventy-two subsidiaries. Without the structure of subsidiaries to operate services for National Express the firm now had to enter contracting agreements with private sector operators.

On 14 July 1986, National Holidays was sold to Pleasurama. National Travel East was sold to ATL Holdings in January 1987. A management buyout of National Express on 17 March 1988 completed the transition to private sector ownership and National Travelworld was sold a week later to Badgerline. Victoria coach station was purchased by London Regional Transport. All the NBC companies had been sold by 1988, and the NBC was then officially dissolved by the Secretary of State.

Nationally, the deregulation of bus operations in 1985 was not a smooth transition and led to both confusion for passengers and wasteful duplication of services, leading to more congestion. Crucially the competitive bus market did not lead to lower fares and more passengers using buses. Many of these new private sector bus companies purchased and ran coach trips and coach holidays, while many coach operators started to run their own bus services and school bus services became available for highly competitive contracting opportunities.

In the summer of 1987, Heather McDonald took up a summer job selling tickets for National Express at the Bullring in Birmingham. She quickly discovered she loved the industry and was soon working as a hostess on board the Rapide services. At just twenty-three, Heather became the first female station inspector – and the youngest. As part of the firm's 40th birthday celebration, *Birmingham Mail* featured Heather's story.

She recalls one driver questioning how she could be an inspector without ever driving a coach. Heather took a week off and enrolled on a driver training course. She was soon driving coaches – something that impressed her colleagues, but still attracted the wrong sort of comments from passengers about having a female driver.

By 2012 Heather had worked for National Express for twenty-five years and was Head of Coach Stations:

> When I started driving there was just me and one other female driver and now I look round and there are scores – it's amazing to think I was one of the first. The coaches are also radically different too. When I started there was no power steering even, now they benefit from the latest state of the art technology including real-time travel information and, driver alcohol testing systems ... I could never have guessed a simple summer job would end up changing my life.

Heather retired at the end of 2021, after thirty-five years' service.

444 LEICESTER - BOURNEMOUTH

	All Journeys		
	Inter	Cum.	RBG
Leicester	-	-	-
Northampton	37	37	-
Milton Keynes	16	53	-
Bletchley	5	58	-
Dunstable	12	70	-
Luton	6	76	-
Bournemouth	136	212	-

450 LONDON - NOTTINGHAM - ALFRETON/MANSFIELD/RETFORD

	All Journeys (except -----)			Ex London 1630 / Ex Alfreton 0725			Ex London 1800 / Ex Kirkby 0820		
	Inter	Cum.	RBG	Inter	Cum.	RBG	Inter	Cum.	RBG
London Victoria	-	-	-	-	-	-	-	-	-
Golders Green	9	9	-	9	9	-	9	9	-
Nottingham	122	131	-	122	131	-	122	131	-
Ilkeston	-	-	-	7	138	-	-	-	-
Alfreton	-	-	-	11	149	-	-	-	-
Mansfield	15	146	-	-	-	-	15	146	-
Sutton-in-Ashfield	-	-	-	-	-	-	-	-	-
Kirkby-in-Ashfield	-	-	-	-	-	-	3	149	-
Worksop	14	160	10	-	-	-	5	154	-
Retford	8	168	-	-	-	-	-	-	-

32

Mileage charts from the *Mileage Information Book* of 26 April 1987 to 31 October 1987. (National Express Archive)

5

1988–92: Acquisitions and Disposals

London Country Berkhof built on a Leyland Tiger BTL10 chassis in London Express livery. (Keith A. Jenkinson).

Now in private ownership, the business could start to develop a new strategy for growth and success. The new operation quickly acquired Crosville Wales and then obtained Eurolines from Grey-Green. Eurolines operated a successful London to Paris and a London to Amsterdam route. A partnership with Thandi Coaches in 1989 to create a Thandi Express as a specialist Asian coach travel business was unsuccessful, but this didn't deter the new management team, and several further acquisitions and partnerships followed in the same year.

1998 was also the year that driver Brian Chambers made it into the headlines for the first time. On the second occasion he was celebrating his retirement from National Express contractor Edwards after fifty-four years. He started working in the bus and coach industry as a tour driver for National Holidays and had driven for both Eurolines and National Express before being promoted to Controller in 1991 for South Wales Transport, First and Edwards Coaches of South Wales in the Swansea depot.

It was his trip on the 549 from Haverfordwest, South Wales, to Scotland on 21 December 1988 that made headlines for the first time. This was the day of the Lockerbie bombing. The coach he was driving was due to leave Carlisle at 18:25 and would travel along the A74 towards Glasgow. The hostess had notified Brian that they had run out of bread to serve customers sandwiches, so Brian made the decision to stop in a local shop to buy a loaf in the interests of customer satisfaction.

Running a few minutes late as a result, heading north and in the vicinity of Lockerbie, Brian and the customers heard an enormous bang coupled with a large flash. The road ahead came to a standstill. After a period of waiting, a car also stuck in the congestion notified Brian and other customers what had happened after listening to the car radio as the news broke. Had Brian not stopped for bread and been delayed, he could have been on the stretch of road ahead affected by the plane crash, which happened just after 7 p.m. – just over 30 minutes' drive from Carlisle.

The debris of Pan Am Flight 103 partially fell on the road and caused several fatalities. Knowing the road was likely to be closed for a considerable time, Brian walked to the Queens Hotel close by and asked whether the customers could be accommodated for the night. There were only ten rooms available, which Brian took, as the alternative was to sleep on the coach. Brian was able to turn the coach on the road and drive to the hotel. All customers were thankful for the actions Brian took, some even giving blood to donate to anyone injured if required. A loaf of bread saved Brian and his customers' lives on the National Express 549 service.

Another story that Brian recalls is a Eurolines journey from Waterford towards South Wales. He was flagged down by a police officer in New Ross, who notified Brian that the boot door was open and at least half of the luggage had been thrown out. A police car had picked up the lost bags and caught up with the coach. In Fishguard Harbour at the time, all coaches had to be unloaded so that full security checks could be completed. Thankfully and much to Brian's relief, no items were missing.

Brian saw many changes over the years. The best coach that he had ever driven was the Volvo Levante, most different to the vehicle in which he passed his PCV test – a 'crash boxed' bus.

Brian looked forward to not being woken up by the alarm clock. He said that his current alarm clock is much smaller than the one that he took with him on his first night away with work in London. He was staying in a room with seven other National Express drivers and was the first driver out on duty. To ensure not to be late, he made sure to set his clock with a massive set of chiming bells, much to the dismay of the other drivers who woke up at its sound!

It was on 20 March 1989 that the firm's first purpose-built coach was launched: the Plaxton Paramount-based Expressliner, built on a Volvo B10M chassis. This vehicle set the standards for the new Rapide brand and was made available to contractors through newly formed National Expressliners Ltd, a joint venture between National Express and Plaxton Roadlease.

A later version of this vehicle was released for non-Rapide services that retained the toilet but replaced the servery with three further seats. This was undoubtedly a successful vehicle and helped Plaxton to compete against European competitors, with operators contractually obliged to use these new vehicles. However, this took time and there was still, two years later, a wide selection of older vehicles carrying Rapide branding, including Plaxton and Duple 425s, Duple 430s, Neoplan Jetliners, MCW Metroliners, older Paramounts, Jonckheere's and Setras. In addition to these single-deckers, a number of Neoplan Skyliners, Plaxton Paramount 4500s (these are built on Skyliner frames) and VanHool Astrobel double-deckers were used on Rapide services. These were not replaced with the Expressliner.

By 1991 things were changing again. 25 per cent of National Express was purchased by Drawlane Transport Group and a consortium of London-based investment companies purchased the other 75 per cent. The new ownership team then floated the business on the London stock market on 1 December 1992 for a price of 165p per share.

Expressliner brochure, highlighting new design features.

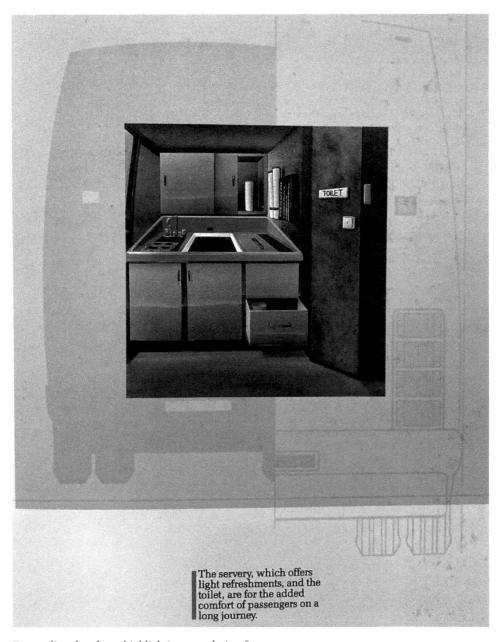

The servery, which offers light refreshments, and the toilet, are for the added comfort of passengers on a long journey.

Expressliner brochure, highlighting new design features.

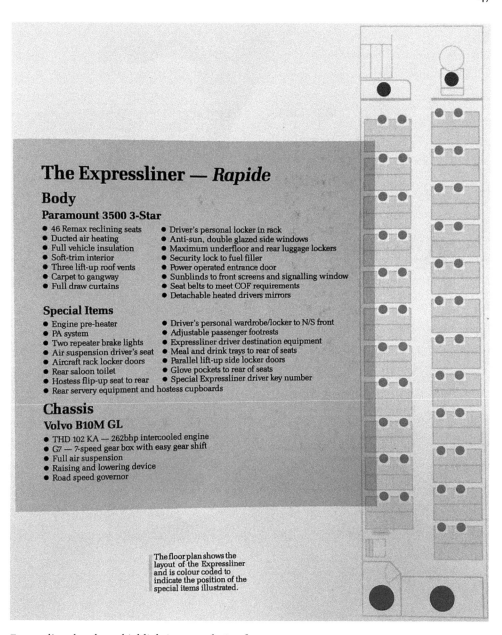

The Expressliner — *Rapide*

Body

Paramount 3500 3-Star

- 46 Remax reclining seats
- Ducted air heating
- Full vehicle insulation
- Soft-trim interior
- Three lift-up roof vents
- Carpet to gangway
- Full draw curtains
- Driver's personal locker in rack
- Anti-sun, double glazed side windows
- Maximum underfloor and rear luggage lockers
- Security lock to fuel filler
- Power operated entrance door
- Sunblinds to front screens and signalling window
- Seat belts to meet COF requirements
- Detachable heated drivers mirrors

Special Items

- Engine pre-heater
- PA system
- Two repeater brake lights
- Air suspension driver's seat
- Aircraft rack locker doors
- Rear saloon toilet
- Hostess flip-up seat to rear
- Rear servery equipment and hostess cupboards
- Driver's personal wardrobe/locker to N/S front
- Adjustable passenger footrests
- Expressliner driver destination equipment
- Meal and drink trays to rear of seats
- Parallel lift-up side locker doors
- Glove pockets to rear of seats
- Special Expressliner driver key number

Chassis

Volvo B10M GL

- THD 102 KA — 262bhp intercooled engine
- G7 — 7-speed gear box with easy gear shift
- Full air suspension
- Raising and lowering device
- Road speed governor

The floor plan shows the layout of the Expressliner and is colour coded to indicate the position of the special items illustrated.

Expressliner brochure, highlighting new design features.

The National Expressliner

Coaching is now a highly competitive business with customers demanding standards of safety, comfort and reliability comparable with private cars and aircraft.

With over 900 coaches in its distinctive white, red and blue colours National Express provides the largest network in Europe. The Company, which was privatised in March 1988, serves over 1500 cities, towns and villages nationwide and carries 15 million passengers a year.

National Express is determined to set new standards and ensure that its passengers are offered consistent quality.

Staff Quality

Every aspect of the Company is being geared to quality; from the telephone enquiry clerk and the Area Manager, to the coach drivers who ensure safety and comfort and the hostesses who see to the passengers' every need. All must be highly trained customer orientated professionals.

Vehicle Quality

Now, the **Expressliner** is launched to ensure that all the vehicles flying the National Express flag will enhance the Company's reputation for quality. National Express have chosen **Volvo** for the running gear and **Plaxton** for the coachwork to ensure that standards of comfort, safety and style are the best available, whilst keeping running costs to a minimum.

Innovation

National Express in conjunction with Roadlease Bus & Coach will provide options for leasing and operating these vehicles.

Innovative packs include contract maintenance arrangements specially designed to meet the exacting requirements of the National Express contractor.

Profit

The **Expressliner** is designed and engineered to provide National Express and the operator with a competitive, effective, realistic and profitable package for the 1990s and beyond.

Meal and drinks trays for the convenience of passengers who wish to enjoy the refreshments offered at the servery.

Expressliner brochure, highlighting new design features. (National Express Archive)

Above: Promotional images for the Rapide service, 1990. (National Express Archive)

Right: Promotional images for the Rapide service, 1990. (National Express Archive)

Promotional images for the Rapide service, 1990. (National Express Archive)

6

The 1990s: Life as a PLC

The new business was valued at £60 million. The firm's investment prospectus made clear that the objectives were to refocus and improve the profitability of the core business, developing new products and services within the existing operations and acquiring new businesses with strong financial viability.

NATIONAL EXPRESS » **CALEDONIAN EXPRESS** »

EXPRESS VIEWS

The bi-monthly magazine for all National Express & Caledonian Express Staff   No. 24.   Christmas 1990

NATIONAL CONTROL HUB OPENS IN BIRMINGHAM

Control of the National Express and Caledonian Express coach network has been centralised following the opening last month of the new Operations Control Centre (OCC) in Birmingham.

Located at National Express Headquarters at Ensign Court, the OCC, under the management of Operations Director Jim Cressey, is now responsible for the day-to-day control of the National Express and Caledonian Express coach network throughout England, Scotland and Wales.

It has been designed to not only respond quickly to problems as and when they arise but also to look ahead and to plan for the major traffic peaks that occur at Christmas, Easter and other national and local holiday periods.

The opening of the OCC, which took place at 2230 on 20 November, has brought an immediate benefit to operating staff with the introduction of a single 24-hour help-line (021-625 1273) and a 24-hour emergency telephone line for customers (021-625 1278).

Regional changes

The opening of the OCC is at the forefront of a major reorganisation which has seen the old regional structure of seven operational areas replaced by four geographical regions, Caledonian, North, Central and South.

Each of the three English regions has its own General Manager, Commercial Manager, Service Manager, Business Development Manager, Agency Manager and Quality and Training Officer. Caledonian comprises a General Manager, Commercial Manager and a Quality and Training Officer.

The split of the previous area sales between Business Development and Agency servicing is designed to exploit new opportunities whilst maintaining the agency network and service. "The Agency Managers will be running our network of 2500 appointed agents to ensure that we continue to offer an unrivalled network of outlets for our products and services" said Marketing Director, Bernard Davis. "The new Business Development Managers will be exploring the opportunities for bringing new business to the Company as well as promoting our extensive range of facilities".

The OCC swings into action on day one with (l-r) Peter Kennedy, Lesley Corry, Cliff Essex, Paul Randle, Fred Wint and Martin Canning keeping the network running.

Staff newsletter from the 1990s. (National Express Archive)

Express News, National
Express magazines, from
the 1990s.

As a result, life as a PLC began with some further restructuring and reorganisation of various business activities, positioning the firm for future growth. While senior management looked at strategic planning, passengers were about to see a number of changes to services.

In 1992 smoking was banned on board all National Express coaches. On-board television was phased out later in the decade. A number of sales and acquisitions positioned the business to purchase East Midlands Airport in 1995.

In 1995 toy manufacturer Corgi launched 'The Original Omnibus', a range of 1/76 (OO gauge) scale model coaches, many presented in National Express livery, joining the array of other models produced by Corgi and other manufacturers.

Some of the more interesting acquisitions of this period included the 1996 purchase of West Midlands Travel and FlightLink, a service that operator Flights of Birmingham had developed earlier in the decade, offering express routes between Birmingham, Heathrow and Gatwick service. After the business was acquired the service continued to operate under the Flightlink brand and was still operated by Flights.

FlightLink-liveried Plaxton Premiere with National Express branding.

Driving the FlightLink service, double crewed and with a hostess, driver Adrian Lees recalls some particularly unusual luggage requests. Adrian recalls a passenger embarking in Birmingham with a Morris Minor gearbox, who simply wouldn't accept his package was, by any definition, air freight. Others wanted to bring unusual gifts and fruit on-board at Heathrow. One item of luggage contained some spider eggs. Stored close to the rear of the coach luggage hold, near the engine where it was warm, these eggs hatched. Posing a genuine threat to native species, Flights had no choice but to take the vehicle out of service for fumigation, with the vehicle spending three days wrapped in cling film.

In 1996 National Express went online, launching www.nationalexpress.com.

At the end of the decade new company Airlinks the Airport Operator was created to manage all airport related travel under the Flightlink, Jetlink and Speedlink brands. Airlinks also purchased Heathrow-based Silverwing Transport Services fleet Cambridge Coach Services. This ensured that Airlinks was now the largest operator of both scheduled and contract services to British Airports Authority Ltd (BAA) and other airline operators.

1993 VanHool Alizee in Speedlink livery. (National Express Archive)

2000 Vanhool Coach in Jetlink livery with 'Go By Coach' branding. (National Express Archive)

It is also worth noting the firm's interest in international growth, acquiring Durham School Services in 1998. Within two years National Express had become one of the top three US school bus operators.

In 1999 the business purchased coach operators and secured rail contracts in Australia. This was also the year that Northern Irish band the Divine Comedy released 'National Express', their third single from their sixth album, *Fin de Siecle*. The song reached number 8 in the UK singles chart. It was inspired by lead singer Neil Hannon's trips aboard a National Express coach. Hannon, who lived in London at the time, used National Express to visit his older brother in Tiverton.

National Express are a large player in the US, operating more than 22,500 school buses and serving more than 550 school districts in thirty-three states and three provinces. The operation transports more than 1.3 million students on a daily basis, using vehicles such as this yellow Bluebird. This is on top of operating a fleet of motor coaches that work transit and shuttle services.

7

The 2000s: The New Millennium

The new millennium began with the final phasing out of the Rapide service – demand for on-board food and drink having been declining for a number of years as passengers increasingly brought their own. A new Plaxton-bodied Expressliner was launched in 2001, which offered contractors more mechanical options and was available with a wheelchair lift as an option. To improve the image of coaching once again, the early 2000s also saw the introduction of the sportier-looking Scania Irizar PB to the National Express fleets (these featured leather seats).

Although the firm made a number of acquisitions early in the decade, including purchasing London United's Airbus Service, Skills of Nottingham's Brighton services and Capital Logistics (purchased from Tellings Golden Miller) much of the first decade was spent focussing on the US and rail business.

In late 2004 National Express Television (NXTV) was launched, showing episodes of UK television series from ITV and BBC including *Top Gear*, *My Family* and *Touch of Frost* and promoted as 'Television shows as you board the coach'. These were played through a dashboard-mounted DVD system and shown on small monitors that rotated down from the overhead luggage compartments. To listen, passengers needed to buy headphones from vending machines at major stations and from on-board vendors before each journey. The sale of headphones was an important part of the business model, but the on-board headphone jacks were standard sized, so passengers realised they could use their own headphones. The iPod was also gaining popularity at this time so not everyone was interested in the offer and a limited range of repeated content led to the service being wound down in 2006. The last few months saw headphones given away for free.

The most significant development was the design and development of the Caetano Levante (see Chapter 8), which was launched in 2006 with front door wheelchair access – perhaps the biggest vehicle fleet news.

National Express UK

National Express is the leading provider of travel solutions in the UK

Coaches

The UK's largest coach network

The most comfortable and reliable coach services in the UK and Europe, offering great value for money and much more.

- National Express Coaches
- Airlinks
- Eurolines
- Kings Ferry

Trains

Fast and frequent passenger services

Direct and convenient passenger rail links including the UK's premier intercity train service linking the capital cities of England and Scotland.

- National Express East Coast
- National Express c2c
- National Express East Anglia
- Stansted Express

Buses

Regular local bus services

High frequency local bus services operating in major cities across the South East, the Midlands and Scotland.

- National Express London
- National Express Surrey
- National Express West Midlands
- National Express Coventry
- National Express Dundee
- Midland Metro

This brochure excerpt shows the breadth of UK travel services offered by National Express around 2009. (National Express Archive)

8

The Caetano Levante Story

> The brief from National Express was an easy access vehicle for schedule 1 of the Disability Discrimination Act with the wow factor.
>
> Caetano.co.uk

National Express have had a long-standing commitment to improving accessibility. In 1985 the business sponsored *Door to Door – A Guide For Disabled People*, a booklet that provided information on every aspect of transport and mobility. One million copies were produced, supported with an audio cassette for visually impaired users. An accompanying film features National Travelworld's High Holborn office and a disabled passenger boarding a Rapide coach at Victoria coach station.

In 2004 the UK distributor for Portuguese manufacturer Salvador Caetano contacted National Express to explore potential sales opportunities. This was at a time when National Express were contemplating how they could ensure their vehicles were all compliant with the new Disability Discrimination Act. The only solution available had been the addition of a wheelchair lift mounted at a specially fitted centre door. This was impractical in chevron spaces in coach parks, time consuming to operate and impacted on the overall layout and design of the coach. Creating a solution which facilitated access through the front door of the coach would be an incredible innovation, and a challenge that the team at Caetano were ready to embrace.

National Express Plaxton Paragon with a standard wheelchair-access solution. (Keith A. Jenkinson)

In conversation with National Express, Caetano Group Sales Manager Richard Hunter described a normal coach wheelchair lift in reverse, with more drop than lift, extending out of the coach passenger door and lifting the wheelchair to the floor height of the coach interior. While the concept was easy to explain, it was going to prove harder to implement. Hydraulic lift manufacturers such as those developing tail lifts were ideally placed to assist but were not interested in helping develop a solution due to the low sales volumes in the UK coach market. However, a chance conversation led to Oldbury-based Passenger Lift Services (PLS) expressing interest in working with Caetano to create a solution. It was their Engineering Director who reformatted the lift to work in conjunction with a new innovation, conceived with Caetano, the Magic Floor. It was this moving floor element that provided the connection between the lift and the saloon and allowed wheelchairs to clear the last hurdle – the step into the saloon. This feature was the key element when it came to naming the new coach, with *levante* being the Portuguese for 'riser'.

The project required significant re-engineering in Portugal, widening the doors and extending the steering shaft. Wheelchair spaces also needed to be located at the front of the vehicle where two pedestal mounted seats are positioned instead of the standard fixed double seating arrangement.

Initially available only on a Volvo B12B chassis, from 2007 operators could also specify a Scania K340 with single or twin rear axles.

Levante 1 cab – driver comfort is critical for delivering great service. (Route One)

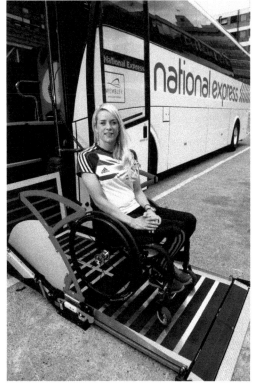

Above: An early Levante 1 on Glastonbury Festival work in 2014 – its eighth year working for National Express. It's believed that this vehicle, FH06 EBM, wore the registration plate FJ07 DWD in a photoshoot to launch the Connector Bar livery on 25 September 2007 – slightly different to what became the standard. (Simon Ingham)

Left: In 2012 Paralympian wheelchair rugby player and athlete Josie Pearson marked the 10th anniversary of the first ever platform lift fitted to a National Express coach in the UK. (National Express)

Caetano Levante II with lift in operation. (National Express)

After their life on the National Express network, Levantes have appeared in the liveries of many other operators. This was uncommon when they were first introduced in the UK, with National Express being the only recipient of the type when new. This coach was new to Bennetts Coaches of Gloucester for the National Express 444 service (Gloucester–London), but has now been reallocated to the private hire and work. (Steve Butler)

Work started in 2012 on the design of the Levante II. Developments were based on feedback from passengers, drivers and operators and covered all aspects of the vehicle operation, from cost reduction to improved comfort. Jorge Guedes, the engineer who led the design of the original Levante, once again took the lead, working in partnership with Almadesign. The updated vehicles were a significant upgrade.

The Levante 3

The design brief for the new vehicle focussed on safety and efficiency, together with planning for the vehicles second life. The vehicles also needed to be able to cope with 22-hour days and mileages of 2.4m km on lease.

This time the project was led by Caetano engineer Rui Rodrigues, again with Almadesign as partners. The first two vehicles were built at 15 m long to maximise the passenger and luggage capacity; however, following consultation with operators the subsequent vehicles were reduced in length to allay concerns about manoeuvrability and the potential increase in collision damage.

Left: Scania prototype under construction at Caetano in Gaia Nova, June 2017. (Richard Ball/ National Express)

Below: Front three-quarter view of a Volvo chassis under construction. (Richard Ball/ National Express)

A Levante 3 cab. The driver's comfort is a top priority for National Express to ensure safety and reduce fatigue. The result is a redesigned dash, with the most used switches nearer the centre, an improved view through the new screen layout and slightly larger mirror views. (National Express)

Considerable time was invested in redesigning key features for passenger comfort, operator usability and second life use. The rear toilet has been redesigned to ensure the floor-mounted cubicle was easy to maintain and clean, with a soft-close sliding door and a two-stage fan to extract air from the toilet. This redesign was combined with a negative pressure setup in the cubicle to ensure that, compared with the pressurised saloon, when the door is opened, air flows into rather than out of the cubicle. The cubicle was also designed so it can be dismantled and removed through the rear emergency door. Retrofit panels are already in stock to recreate the saloon, adding four seats to make a sixty-three-seater. Passenger comfort is also much improved with the installation of underfloor heating, which is a market first, improving legroom and providing better heat distribution throughout the vehicle.

In September 2017 the Levante III was launched onto the National Express with prototypes being built for National Express contractors Edwards Coaches on a Volvo B11R chassis and Skills Coaches on a Scania chassis.

Caetano Design Language, 1997–2020. (Almadesign)

Caetano Design Language, 1997–2020. (Almadesign)

Caetano Design Language, 1997–2020. (Almadesign)

Right: The front step, which hides the lift equipment and features limited branding for second life adaptation.

Below: Jorge Guedes (right), engineer at Caetano and responsible for bringing the Levante III to life, with Richard Ball (National Express) at the UK press launch of Caetano UK.

9

Coach Stations

The coach station has always been an important feature of the National Express service, and the passenger experience here is just as important as the on-board service. The fact that British Coachways' failure was, in part at least, a result of the poor-quality terminus in London, illustrates this point well.

In 1934, the main operational base for Associated Motorways was the new St Margaret's Road coach station in Cheltenham, which had been built by Black & White Motorways in 1932. However, the infrastructure needs of the growing coach industry in the interwar years had become a major issue for both operators and passengers. While bus companies in large conurbations developed new facilities, bus garages and bus stops, coach operators had antiquated arrangements for picking up their passengers, meeting outside public houses or in the local square. In response, the London Coastal Coaches consortium built the imposing art deco Victoria coach station in London in 1932.

Victoria coach station in 1948. (National Express Archive)

Victoria coach station in 1961.
(National Express Archive)

Not all facilities were planned or designed as coach passenger interchanges, however. The Midland Red bus depot at Spencer House, which was built in 1929, had never been designed with passengers in mind. As Midland Red, and its successor Midland Red West, started to operate longer distance routes they needed somewhere for passengers to embark on their journeys. Many people remember the dark and dingy fume-filled space fondly as they waited for coaches to take them to meet friends, away on holiday or for arrivals coming to Birmingham.

While the 1950s and 1960s were described as the golden age of coach travel, this really reflects a nostalgia for tourist travel and sightseeing. Long-distance scheduled services were seen somewhat differently. Many coach stations in the 1960s and 1970s, like Skelhorne Street in Liverpool and Digbeth in Birmingham, had developed reputations as dismal, chaotic environments, which contributed to the poor image of long-distance coach travel in the eyes of the traveling public.

As more attention was paid to the customer experience before the journey, National Express started to invest in the coach station experience. Today National Express are the sole operators for Southampton, Birmingham, Cardiff, Plymouth, Leeds and Manchester coach stations.

Manchester coach station, which first opened in 1950 was built around three platform islands with shelters, before being redesigned in 1963 with the addition of a multistorey coach park. However, the station earned an unenviable reputation for being cold, windy, and generally miserable. After a full rebuild the new station opened in 2002.

Moor Lane, Digbeth, before Midland Red started construction. (National Express Archive)

Digbeth bus depot, 1929.

The opening of Manchester coach station, 2002. (National Express Archive)

A typical scene from Victoria coach station: a line-up of five Caetano Levantes and two Plaxton Elites awaiting to depart the terminal building. Various 'super-rears' on display. (Simon Ingham)

Heathrow Central bus station first opened in 1950. This large station serves terminals 2 and 3, and is the UK's busiest bus and coach station with 1,600 services every day to 1,000 destinations. To improve the passenger experience here, a new inflatable roof was installed in 2005, creating a comfortable space for passengers waiting to board their coach.

Digbeth Becomes Home

In its early days National Express headquarters were based at the Midland Red Offices on Waterworks Road in Edgbaston, before the firm moved to Ensign Court in Edgbaston. Although Digbeth became the focus for coach operations for National Express in 1984, the firms' head office remained in Edgbaston for around thirty years, before relocating to No. 1 Hagley Road.

Plans for a major regeneration of Birmingham city centre provided an opportunity for urban planners to think again about the city's infrastructure, and that initially included a proposal to move the coach station to Great Charles Street. The completion of other projects, including the Bullring, meant that the Digbeth location was now close to the re-emerging heart of the city. A decision was taken to demolish the old structure and build a new coach station on the same site.

Designed by SBS Architects, planning permission was granted in 2007. For two years coach operations were managed from a temporary site in Oxford Street named Birmingham Central coach station. The new station, on completion, was awarded a BREEAM Excellent rating for its sustainable design and construction.

2016 saw the opening of the new Plymouth coach station. Managed by National Express, the £4.85 million development has seven bays and operates real-time passenger information, a staffed ticket office, a café and various amenities, including toilets, cycle parking and ticket vending machines.

The new £15 million coach station was reopened in 2009 by Fabio Capello, the then-current England national football team's manager. (National Express)

Birmingham's new coach station. (National Express)

Birmingham's new coach station. (National Express)

Birmingham's new coach station. (National Express)

Plymouth coach station.

'Plymouth by Aleisha'. The opening was celebrated with a design competition that saw the winner's artwork applied to a Caetano Levante.

When Oluwatosin Adejumo went into labour at Victoria coach station, while saying goodbye to her sister and toddler son with her husband Peter Kofoworola, it was up to coach station staff to lend a hand until paramedics arrived. The baby born on the floor at Victoria coach station was reunited with the staff who helped deliver her after they launched an appeal to track her down. Unsurprisingly, perhaps, the newest member of the family has been named Victoria.

10

Safety Critical

Safety has been an important part of the National Express brand, with the organisation often leading the sector.

In 2016 National Express partnered with Highways England to support their latest road safety initiative. The 'Don't be a Space Invader – stay safe, stay back' campaign used the well-known *Space Invaders* video game character to alert drivers to the anti-social nature and risks of tailgating. The retro 'Space Invaders' poster featured on twelve coach rears and stickers have been added to bumpers of the remaining 500-plus fleet of vehicles to remind people travelling at speed that tailgating is dangerous.

> This is a great opportunity to highlight this important safety issue. As the UK's largest coach operator, we experience tailgating of our vehicles and fully endorse the message to not be a Space Invader and leave enough space. We focus on safe driving through a combination of training and technology and fully support Highways England in urging all road users to not practise this unsafe behaviour.
>
> Chris Hardy, Managing Director, National Express UK Coach

A retro 'Space Invaders' poster featured on a coach rear as part of a Highways England campaign to remind people traveling at speed that tailgating is dangerous. (National Express)

Other innovations include the Alcolock system (which prevents drivers from starting a vehicle's engine until they pass an alcohol breathalyser test), built-in cameras to monitor driver standards, on-board CCTV and a Traffilog tracking system to monitor vehicle speed and punctuality to ensure customers are given the best possible service.

In 2019 National Express was awarded the British Safety Council's Sword of Honour in recognition of its excellent health and safety management standards – one of only eighty-five firms nationally to secure the award that year and the only organisation in the transport sector to achieve the accolade for five consecutive years. The award followed a successful five-star result from the council's thirteen-day health and safety audit alongside ISO 45001 certification – an international standard that specifies requirements for an occupational health and safety (OH&S) management system.

In 2021 the business won a RoSPA Gold Award for its commitment to safety.

11

A Modern Global Business

Always keen to support good causes and special events, National Express have, in recent years, wrapped vehicles in promotional liveries to celebrate events as diverse as Armed Forces Day, the Commonwealth Games and the Olympics.

Just before the business celebrated its 40th birthday in 2012, it had launched a 24/7 London to Dover route and introduced Wi-Fi on the London to Stansted route. This would later be rolled out across the entire fleet.

This was also the year the National Express Foundation was created to help tackle the challenges faced by young people living in inner cities. It does this through the provision of grants to charitable and community groups for projects that support young people to enjoy positive and developmental activities and promote cross-community cohesion and understanding. Now in its tenth year, the National Express Foundation has helped around 25,000 young people to succeed in life.

National Express is an official partner of the Royal British Legion. In 2013, it was the first company to sign up to an Armed Forces Covenant to formally recognise the significant contribution of the Armed Forces to the company and the country. This commitment was renewed in 2018 for a further five years, and offers, among other benefits, guaranteed

FJ10 EZT of Silverdale wearing it's 'Irish' take on the National Express livery, promoting connections to Dublin, Belfast and Cork. Seen in Victoria coach station in June 2015. (Simon Ingham)

Caetano Levante wrapped for the Commonwealth Games. (Simon Ingham)

Dean Finch, National Express Group Chief Executive, with the Rt Hon Tobias Ellwood MP, Minister for Defence People and Veterans, at an event at Horse Guards Parade to mark the signing of a new Armed Forces Covenant.

interviews to service leavers, and their spouses and families, for all National Express roles across coach and bus operations. Staff in the reserve forces are given ten days extra leave and all service leavers can access discounted travel, and free bus travel to families visiting soldiers at the Military Hospital at the QE in Birmingham.

A partnership with RyanAir in the same year allowed passengers to book coach transfers and flights at the same time, an agreement which was later extended to EasyJet and to Wizz Air in 2014. In the same year an agreement was also made with the Post Office to sell tickets for National Express services.

National Express partnered with British Airways to provide staff shuttles to their Waterside-registered office. Resting Enviro 200s wearing both British Airways and National Express logos are seen at this location in October 2016. (Simon Ingham)

An unusual vehicle to see in National Express livery. This Volvo B11 Sunsundegui, operated by Excalibur, was helping out on Stansted Airport services in 2016. (Simon Ingham)

FJ13 EAO wearing its overall wrap for the 2015 Pride of Britain Awards. It is seen turning into Victoria coach station arrivals, having completed a 410 service. (Simon Ingham)

Driver Andy Muskett recalls the time in 2014 he made it into the *Daily Mail* after finding a silver tabby cat hiding above his coach's fuel tank. Christened Diesel, the cat had travelled 100 miles from Westward Ho! and it was only when driver Andy heard meowing as he unloaded passengers' luggage at Bristol that he realised he had a stowaway. Passengers were transferred to another vehicle to continue their journey to Grimsby while Andy spent the evening coaxing the terrified cat out from above the fuel tank with the help of engineer Andy Teagle. Diesel had no collar or microchip so was taken back to the depot for some food and drink.

Back in the UK, 2016 saw the acquisition of coach operator Clarkes of London. As with Kings Ferry these vehicles have continued to operate under their own livery, though management of the business was handed to the Kings Ferry operation. This was followed in March 2020 by the purchase of Lucketts Group. 2016 also saw the reintroduction of double-deckers with six Caetano Boa Vista vehicles based on the Scania K340. *Boa vista* translates from Portuguese to English as 'good/beautiful view' and relates to the view from the top deck.

The first day of Edwards' Bristol depot operating services, including double-deck Boa Vista on the 040 (Bristol to London). BV66 WPJ (named *Paul* in recognition of a long-serving employee) is reversing off the stand, about to start its London run via Earls Court. Ten such vehicles are on the network, having since been upgraded to incorporate a premium seating offering. The '66' plates were new to National Express-owned operations for Luton Airport services. The four '18' plates were first operated by Edwards. (Simon Ingham)

Premium seating on the Caetano Boa Vista. (National Express)

Paula Russell and Simon Ingham at Cardiff/Caerdydd coach station, Sophia Gardens, in August 2016 showing recognition for the Summer Olympics in Rio. Paula and Simon married in November 2019, after meeting through work. Paula won a Gold award as Young Industry Professional in the UK Coach Awards in her role as Coach Station Manager for Cardiff and Bristol.

Park's of Hamilton engineers posing for a picture, having been awarded a 'Golden Spanner'. The Golden Spanner awards are a symbol of engineering excellence, created to recognise exemplar performance in both reliability and engineering standards. They are genuine 'Snap On' spanners plated in real gold and the metric size indicates the year that the spanner is awarded for, so 16 mm is for 2016. (Simon Ingham)

It is worth noting that in 2017 National Express sold their sole remaining C2C rail franchise to Trenitalia, which represented their complete exit from UK rail operations.

2017 was also an important year for staff. With people always placed at the forefront of the operation, National Express pledged to pay all of its UK employees the voluntary, higher real living wage. At the time it was the largest private sector employer in both the West Midlands and UK public transport to be officially recognised by the Living Wage Foundation.

The move benefitted more than 240 employees, most of whom worked in the UK coach business. As well as pledging to pay its UK staff the real living wage, National Express ensured all agency and contracted staff were included in this increase and worked with its partner operators to ensure their employees were also paid the real living wage by 2020. The move has a real impact on employees who have explained the difference it makes. Customer Service Advisor Ashley, based at Birmingham coach station, said: 'Being paid the real living wage is benefitting me a lot. At the moment I'm living with my parents and the increase is helping me save for my future home.' Philip, an Administrator with National Express West Midlands, said:

> Without being on the real living wage, my partner and I could have really struggled with getting our mortgage, buying a house and being able to start a family. It's refreshing to have an employer who gives me the feeling they want to invest in me, my health, my wellbeing and my future – and not just get labour for the cheapest outlay in the short term.

In May 2019, National Express launched a new competition, Driving Design, offering aspiring artists the chance of seeing their work come to life across the side of one of National Express' iconic 14-metre-long coaches for a year. The winner of Driving Design in 2019 was twenty-seven-year-old Sergej Komkov from Hull.

On 6 April 2020, in response to the Covid-19 pandemic, all services were cancelled after numbers were reduced to unsustainable levels. Services restarted on 1 July, delivering around a quarter of the route coverage pre-pandemic, before operations were halted again on 11 January 2021. Limited services resumed on 29 March 2021 and the network has been recovering since this time.

Despite the impact of Covid-19, August 2020 also saw the creation of a new business focusing on the UK holiday and leisure travel market, bringing several brands, including Lucketts and Woods under the single banner of 'National Express Leisure'. This new entity plans to become the number one place to go for holidays and leisure travel by coach with a full range of great value options of ready-made or build-your-own packages.

Artist Sergei Komkov with the Caetano Levante 3 that carries his artwork.

In 2020 National Express completed the purchase of the family-owned Lucketts Group, which includes Lucketts Travel, Coliseum Coaches, Mortons Travel, Solent Coaches and Worthing Coaches, making it the largest coach operator on the south coast, employing 350 people and operating a fleet of 160 coaches and buses.

National Express Leisure will offer the best in convenience and choice along with the great value and high standards of customer service and safety we're already well known for.

John Boughton, Commercial Director at National Express

Current National Express Partners
Ambassador Travel, Great Yarmouth
Bennetts Coaches, Gloucester
Bruce's Coaches, Salsburgh, North Lanarkshire
Chalfont Coaches, Southall and Northampton
Clarkes of London*
Edwards Coaches, Llantwit Fardre and Avonmouth
East Yorkshire, Kingston upon Hull
Galloway European, Mendlesham
Go North East, Chester-le-Street

Kavanagh, Ireland
Lucketts Travel, Fareham*
Solent & Worthing
Llew Jones International, Llanrwst
National Express West Midlands (Walsall)*
National Express South East*
Newbury and District,
Park's Motor Group
Hamilton, Plymouth
Oxford Bus Reading Buses, Reading
Selwyns Travel, Runcorn, Manchester and Leeds
Skills Coaches, Nottingham
Stotts Coaches, Huddersfield
Stagecoach Yorkshire, Barnsley
The Kings Ferry*
Travelstar European, Walsall
Woods Coaches*
Yeomans Canyon Travel, Hereford

In 2020 National Express Coach expanded its network of scheduled airport coach services outside of the UK with a contract award in Ireland, securing a deal to run a high-frequency, cross-city network with Ireland-based Bernard Kavanagh Coaches, a company with a long-standing relationship with National Express, operating the service on their behalf. Launched in March, and then postponed due to Covid-19, before being relaunched in August 2021, Dublin Express operates three routes, up to 24 hours a day, between Dublin Airport and Dublin city centre. A phased expansion of the network will see additional services being added to connect more locations across the city and increase the frequency of airport connections.

Edwards' fleet at the Swansea depot on 15 July 2012 – the day before the business started operating from Swansea. (Edwards Coaches)

Dublin Express service.

12

A Chance Encounter...

Over the years National Express has played its part in a few romances, and some of these have become headline news in their local papers.

In 2011 *Coach Times* reported on the story of Hazel and Leon Czarnceki. It was an ordinary day at work for Hazel, who worked at Canterbury bus station in 1985 when Leon Czarnceki came in to purchase a National Express coach ticket for Glasgow, to see his mother. When he returned, Hazel remembered him, and asked how his mother was. Leon commented on her good memory, and although Hazel was convinced Leon was more interested in her friend, she was persuaded to go for a meal with Leon. When she turned up at work the next day a large bouquet was waiting for her. Just two weeks later the couple were married at Canterbury Registry Office. They had a church blessing ten years later in Chilham, where Hazel grew up and where the couple now live.

In May 2016 *Essex Standard Gazette* reported on the story of Geoff and Patricia Lambert who met on the National Express 250 service from Stansted Airport to Colchester in 2015. Geoff was from Sussex, but lived in New Zealand and was travelling to visit family in

Geoff and Patricia first met on a National Express coach as strangers in 2015 and got married the following year. (National Express)

Colchester. He boarded an earlier coach than planned, having got through customs in record time. Patricia was travelling home to Colchester after a trip to Southend and chose the seat next to Geoff for the extra legroom it afforded. Great conversation followed, and they soon realised each other were single. They exchanged numbers so they could keep in touch while Geoff was in the UK, and they really missed each other when Geoff returned home.

Patricia left her job and emigrated. They married in 2016 in the Bay of Plenty, and their relationship has since been celebrated by National Express with two seats temporarily dedicated to their relationship. The seats were specially commissioned by National Express seat supplier Fainsa and were unveiled by Arron Slater, who was driving the coach on the day of their first meeting.

The *Cynon Valley Leader* celebrated the story of Matt and Gail, who met on a National Express coach when Gail asked if she could use the seat next to Matt. This meant moving the bag he had put there to discourage people! Matt recalls, 'She asked if he could sit next to me to keep an eye on her kids. I moved my bag off the empty seat with a scowl and apparently her first impression of me was that I was "rude"!'

Eventually the pair started a conversation, and Gail said that 'I realised during the course of our conversation that I really liked him and could see myself with him long term, so we exchanged numbers. Then when we changed coaches at Bristol to my disappointment. I wasn't sitting next to him. I texted him to say "are you lonely?" and he said "yes" and I knew he was interested.'

After four months Matt moved from Torquay to Pontypridd to be with Gail, becoming stepdad to her children. They married the following year in Lapland. To celebrate their tenth wedding anniversary National Express gave the couple a pair of coach tickets to go anywhere they want on the UK coach network.

In 2019, Simon and Joanne Jones were celebrating their 25th wedding anniversary and got in touch with the customer service team to share their story. The couple met on a National Express coach thirty years earlier and were offered a trip down memory lane by National Express, who managed to find a coach that was used at the time they met, and also gifted them with a framed timetable from when they travelled.

Joanne was travelling from Manchester to see her family in Crawley and Simon was heading to Gatwick Airport for a holiday to Magaluf. He took the empty seat next to Joanne at the back of the coach.

I remember he was listening to Madonna on his Walkman. It was very loud. The driver made an announcement about a delay and Simon took his headphones off to ask what he had said. We talked the rest of the way to London and exchanged addresses when we got to Victoria. That week I received a postcard from Simon from Magaluf which I still have to this day. A month later we went on our first date and the rest is history.

And it was thanks to National Express that the couple were able to make a long-distance relationship work for the first two years: meeting up every week was only possible by using the coach.

Simon said, 'We are proof that long-distance relationships really can work. We got married five years later and now have two grown-up children that we are very proud of. Sara is twenty-four and working in China and Ben is in his final year at drama school.'

Geoff and Patricia first met on a National Express coach as strangers in 2015 and got married the following year. (National Express)

13

National Express at 50 Years

The milestone of a half century of operations is a big cause for celebration for any company. This is particularly noteworthy given the challenges of a global pandemic that has had a huge impact on travel and transport businesses. National Express was no exception, with services being suspended in both 2020 (March–June) and 2021 (January–March) in response to national lockdowns and reduced demand. Despite this, the business remains the UK's largest coach operator, with over 21 million journeys made in 2019. The numbers for the operation behind this include:

- 500-plus coaches
- Over 2,000 drivers
- 500 destinations including major airports and universities
- 1,800-plus services every day and over 1,900 on Fridays
- An annual mileage in excess of 70 billion

Delivering the greatest possible comfort is more important than ever, with modern coaches averaging just three years old and an on-board experience offering leather seats, air conditioning, USB and power points, CCTV and toilets.

And industry leading, award-winning safety goes beyond the minimum requirement with technology such as the Alcolock system, which doesn't allow the engine to start until the driver has passed an alcohol breathalyser test, speed-monitoring systems and cameras that monitor driver performance.

COP26 has focused minds on the environment and 'levelling up' is high on the agenda. Good transport improves lives – it provides connections and opens up opportunities. Coach travel will be more important than ever before in the future.

Just one coachload of people can keep up to fifty cars off the roads and the average carbon dioxide emissions per passenger per journey is around 1.5 times lower than rail, five times lower than air and six times lower than car travel. Just a 15 per cent increase in coach passenger journeys by British people each year could lead to approximately 47 million fewer cars on the road, saving over a quarter of a million tonnes of carbon dioxide and significantly reducing congestion. Coaches are one of the greenest ways to travel.

National Express is well placed to play its part in the future of travel. All of its vehicles already meet the highest possible engine emission standard (Euro VI) and they have committed to making the fleet zero emission by 2035 – ahead of the UK net zero target of 2050.

Alternative fuels will be the next big leap and it is widely expected that National Express will continue to be a leader in the coach sector and one of the first to trial and ultimately adopt changes in this area.

What is under the bonnet and inside the coach will undoubtedly change, but the much loved red, white and blue National Express looks set to be here for the foreseeable future.

The Caetano Levante 3. (Mike Molloy)

The Caetano Levante 3. (Mike Molloy)

Timeline

1929 – Chapter 1
- Midland Red build a depot in Digbeth
- The 1930 Transport Act comes into force and governs coaching operations nationally
- Victoria coach station is opened in 1932

1968 – Chapter 2
- The 1968 Transport Act is enacted leading to nationalisation of bus and coach services
- National Bus Company (NBC) is formed

1969
- NBC form a joint venture with British Leyland Motor Corporation (25 per cent owner of Bristol and Eastern Coach Works/ ECW) to create the Leyland National

1971
- Frederick Wood appointed Chairman of the National Bus Company

1972
- The majority of scheduled coach services run by the National Bus Company are united under one brand, initially known as 'National'
- Central Activities Group is created

1974 – Chapters 3 and 4
- National Express brand first appears

1976
- National Holidays is established to promote coach tours

1977
- National Holidays becomes part of the National Travel Group and Central Activities Group is disbanded

1980 – Chapter 5
- The 1980 Transport Act leads to deregulation of coach services and the subsequent breakup of the National Bus Company in the late 1980s
- British Coachways consortium launches services

1981
- The first London Rapide service operated in partnership with Trathens
- National Dispatch was launched (a parcels logistics solution in partnership with Marlaway) and partners with TNT to develop a nationwide service
- AirCoach brand created for services from Bristol, Bournemouth and Southampton to Gatwick, and from Cardiff, Bristol and Newport to Heathrow.

1982
- British Coachways cease to operate
- NBC introduce the Dennis Falcon Duple coach for use on Rapide services

1983
- Dedicated fleet of high-specification coaches for National Express introduced based on Leyland Tiger chassis with Plaxton bodywork
- The first inter-urban Rapide Service runs from Manchester to Glasgow
- New brands, including London Crusader, are created
- Supabus is created to act as a marketing agency for government-approved Continental services. Initial routes included the firm's own Irish services and intercontinental services offered by Budget-Bus and Euroways
- National Travelworld created from eighty-four separate travel agents operating within the NBC Group

1984
- Metroliner double-deck coaches introduced for use on both Rapide and non-Rapide National Express services and built in Birmingham
- National Products Group is created

1986
- National Express services became operated by operators under contract
- National Holidays is sold to Pleasurama

1987
- National Travel East sold to ATL Holdings

1988 – Chapter 6
- National Travelworld sold to Badgerline
- Management buyout of National Express
- Acquisition of Crosville Wales and Eurolines

1989
- Partnership with Thandi Coaches to develop a UK network for Asian travellers
- Joint Venture with Shamrock & Rambler to create Dorset Travel Services
- Creation of London Express (short distance feeder services with twice daily connections at London Victoria)

- Acquisitions including:
  - o Amberline, Merseyside to become a subsidiary of Crossville Wales
  - o ATL Holdings (including SUT, Carlton PSV dealership and Yelloway-Trathen)
  - o Stagecoach's Scottish operations then rebranded as Caledonian Express
  - o Euroways London to Alicante route
  - o Wallace Arnold's Barcelona and Paris routes
- Joint venture with West Yorkshire Road Car Company's Yorkshire Voyager Travel Services
- Tayside Travel Services created to manage Caledonian Express
- Sale of SUTs bus operations to Hallam Bus Company (part of the South Yorkshire PTE)
- Launch of the Plaxton Paramount-based Expressliner exclusive to National Express services including Rapide and Caledonian Express.
- Creation of National Expressliners, a joint venture between National Express and Plaxton Roadlease

1990
- Merry-go-Round service introduced between Glasgow and Edinburgh
- London Express discontinued
- Rotherham Travel Services closed
- Amberline was divided up and shared with newly formed National Express-owned Roadmaster Travel Services

1991
- Yorkshire Voyager Travel Services sold
- National Express purchased by Drawlane Transport Group and a consortium of investors
- Speedlink Airport Services purchased from Drawlane
- National Express floated on the London stock market on 1 December 1992 for a price of 165p per share

1992 – Chapter 7
- National Express sold it's 50 per cent share of Trathens Travel Services and Dorset Travel
- Trathens returns to family ownership
- Bournemouth Transport acquired Dorset Travel Services
- Express Travel Services created to take over Roadmaster Travel Services and Tayside Travel Services
- Smoking banned on board all National Express coaches
- 80 per cent stake in the Carlton dealership sold to Stuart Johnson and rebranded as SJ Carlton
- Express Travel of Perth sold to British Bus
- Launch of Expressliner II offering operators a choice of chassis and ownership methods

1993
- Purchase of Scottish Citylink

1994
- Airlinks service introduced to provide airport services
- Purchase of East Midlands Airport
- New Liverpool coach station opened
- Rapide Plus launched from Newcastle-upon-Tyne to London

1995
- Acquisitions including:
  - Yorkshire Express with their direct London to Bradford and Leeds services
  - Bournemouth Airport
  - Highland Country Buses (via Scottish CityLink), a minority stake in West Coast Motors and a 25 per cent stake in Skyeways Coaches
  - West Midlands Travel

1996
- New Leeds coach station opened
- Purchase of Flightlink from Flights of Birmingham
- Awarded two rail franchises: Midland Mainline and Gatwick Express
- Launch of www.nationalexpress.com

1997
- Scottish Citylink is broken up with Highland Country Buses sold back to Rapsons and Citylink sold to London Metroline operators ComfortDelGro
- Acquisitions including:
  - Taybus Services
  - Belgian bus operator, Bronckaers
- HotelHoppa Service launched at Heathrow

1998
- New Southampton coach station opened
- National Express enters the US market with the acquisition of Durham School Services and Crabtree-Harmon

1999
- Airlinks the Airport Operator created to manage all airport-related travel and acquires Heathrow-based Silverwing Transport Services fleet and Cambridge Coach Services fleet
- The Divine Comedy release their third single from their sixth album, 'National Express'
- Purchase of Australia's largest private bus operator, National Bus Company, in May
- Secured the M>Train, M>Tram and V/Line Passenger rail franchises in the Australian state of Victoria in August.

2000 – Chapters 8 and 9
- On-board catering services end
- Final Rapide services cease
- Airbus is purchased and launches high-frequency links between central London and Heathrow, Gatwick and Stansted airports. Existing Jetlink services are merged into the new Airbus brand and timetables
- GoByCoach.com replaces existing coach internet booking sites
- Acquired American operator ATC

2001
- New Plaxton Expressliner
- Acquisitions including:
  - London United's Airbus Service
  - Skills of Nottingham's Brighton services
  - Capital Logistics purchased from Tellings Golden Miller

2002
- The new Manchester coach station opens
- Australian rail franchises handed back

2003
- First accessible coach is introduced on the Bath to London service
- Launch of Megabus in the UK

2004
- National Express TV (NXTV) launched
- London bus operations owned by Tellings Golden Miller rebranded as Travel London
- First e-tickets are introduced

2005
- First SMS tickets introduced
- Tellings Golden Miller acquired and rebranded as Travel London

2006
- NXTV was wound down
- First Caetano Levante fully accessible coach is launched

2007
- National Express Dot-to-Dot launched
- Acquisition of the Kings Ferry
- National Express become the official Wembley Stadium travel partner
- Digbeth coach station closes and moves to a temporary site in Oxford Street, Birmingham

- Acquired Continental Auto, the second-largest bus and coach operator in Spain
- Rebrand launched in November
- InterCity East Coast rail franchise begins

2008
- Dot-to-Dot sold to Corot

2009
- The new Birmingham coach station is officially opened by Fabio Capello
- Launch of Greyhound in the UK

2010
- National Express is announced as a principal sponsor of Commonwealth Games England and official supporter of the team ahead of the games in Glasgow in in 2014
- New Milton Keynes Coachway opens
- Alcolock is introduced on all vehicles

2011 – Chapter 12
- National Express Call Centre opens 24/7
- A new platform allows real time tracking of vehicles by the network control centre

2012
- Wi-Fi introduced on the London to Stansted route
- National Express Foundation created to support young people
- Coachtracker allows passengers to view where their coach is before and during the journey in real time

2013
- National Express Coach is the first UK business to pledge to an Armed Forces Covenant
- Partnership with RyanAir to allow passengers to book coach transfers and flights at the same time
- Agreement with the Post Office to sell tickets for National Express services
- National Express operates Christmas Day services for the first time
- Awarded two regional rail contracts by the Verkehrsverbund Rhein-Ruhr, Zweckverband
- Nahverkehr Rheinland and Zweckverband Nahverkehr Westfalen-Lippe authorities in Germany

2014
- David Soul features in TV advertising campaign
- National Express agrees charity partnership with Canine Partners

2015
- Cardiff bus station closed and National Express operations moved to Sophia Gardens
- National Express partners with Pride of Britain awards to provide coach travel

2016

- National Express is the first UK private transport group to become an accredited Living Wage Foundation employer
- Acquisition of Clarkes of London
- Double-decker coaches reintroduced onto the National Express network
- New Plymouth coach station opens
- Liverpool's Norton Street coach station is closed for redevelopment, with coaches operating from Liverpool One bus station
- Drivecam is introduced on all vehicles
- Launch of the Stay Safe, Stay Back campaign

2017

- HotelHoppa sold to Rotala
- Caetano Levante III launched

2018

- 2018 Armed Forces Covenant is renewed for a further five years to include all National Express UK businesses
- Awarded British Safety Council Sword of Honour
- Partners with Highways England to promote 'Don't be a Space Invader – stay safe, stay back' road safety campaign

2019

- National Express secures first place at the British Quality Foundation's (BQF) annual awards with the UK Excellence Award

2020

- Purchase of Lucketts Group
- Launch of Dublin Express
- National Express pledges for all coaches to be fully zero emission by 2035
- Reduced services restart in June following a twelve-week suspension at the start of the Covid-19 pandemic
- Creation of National Express Leisure

2021

- Restart of services in March following a second suspension in response to the Covid-19 pandemic
- Relaunch of Dublin Express
- Creation of National Express Leisure – a new business focusing on the UK holiday and leisure travel market
- Winner of RoSPA Gold Award for Fleet Safety